Be An Expert!™

Cool Cars

Erin Kelly

Children's Press®

An imprint of Scholastic Inc.

Contents

Know the Names

Be an expert! Get to know the names of these cool cars!

Sports Cars

Here they come.
They are fun to drive!

Porsche 911

Ferrari

Zoom In

Find these parts on the sports cars.

bumper **emblem** **headlight** **spoiler**

Corvette

Limousines

They are long.

Hummer stretch limousine

driver

Expert Fact

The biggest limo ever made had a **hot tub** and four TVs!

Police Cars

Look at the lights on top.

Zoom In

Find these parts on the police car.

sirens   **lights**   **speaker**   **car number**

SUVs

They go off the road!

Jeep Cherokee

Driving It Home

Q: How can an SUV move off the road?

A: Big wheels let it drive over rocks or mud.

Ford Escapade

Tiny Cars

They are so cute!

Fiat 500

Mini Cooper

Expert Fact

Small cars use less **gas** than big cars.

Smart car

Mini Cooper convertible

Minivans

Get in. We all fit!

Chrysler Pacifica

Honda Odyssey

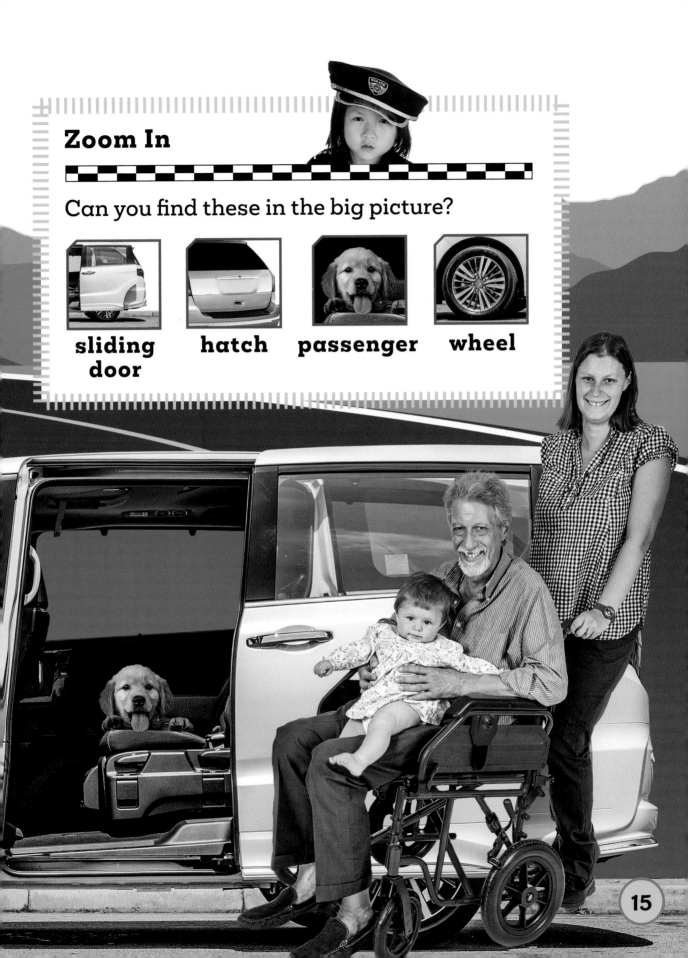

Zoom In

Can you find these in the big picture?

sliding door   **hatch**   **passenger**   **wheel**

Self-Driving Cars

Who is driving? No one!

East

West

Tesla with autopilot

Waymo

Expert Fact

A person tells the car where to go. Then a computer drives it!

Race Cars

They go fast. Zoom!

Indy

Formula 1

Driving It Home

Q: How do you go fast and not crash?

A: I pay attention. And I practice a lot!

NASCAR

All the Cars

Beep, beep. Thanks for the ride!

1.

2.

5.

6.

Expert Quiz

Do you know the names of these cars? Then you are an expert! See if someone else can name them too!

3.

4.

7.

8.

Answers: 1. Minivan. 2. Self-driving car. 3. Tiny car. 4. SUV. 5. Sports car. 6. Limousine. 7. Police car. 8. Race car.

Expert Gear

What do race car drivers wear to stay safe?

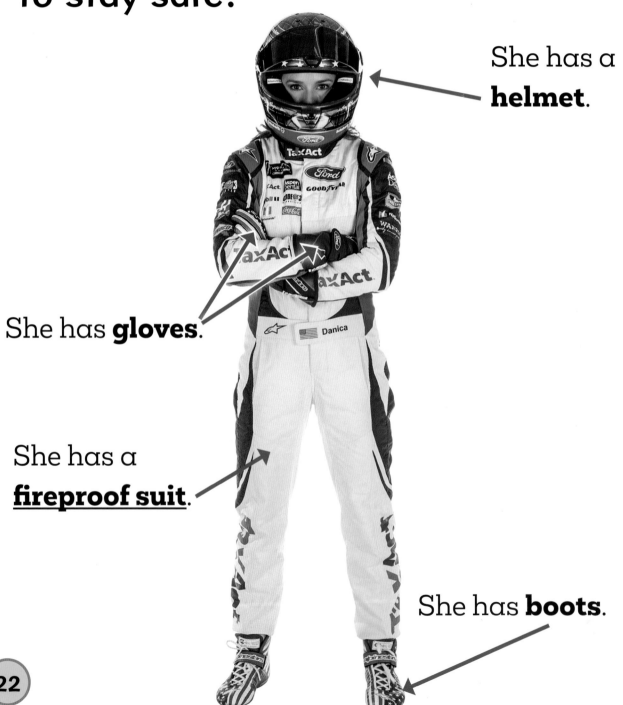

She has a **helmet**.

She has **gloves**.

She has a **fireproof suit**.

She has **boots**.

Glossary

emblem (EHM-bluhm): a marker on a car that lets you know what company made it.

fireproof suit (FIRE-proof soot): a suit that will not catch fire in a crash.

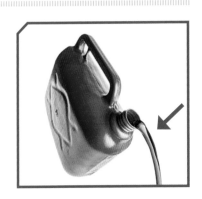

gas (GASS): short for "gasoline," a liquid you put into a car to make it go.

hot tub (HAHT tuhb): a big tub of warm water bubbles.

Index

Library of Congress Cataloging-in-Publication Data
Names: Kelly, Erin Suzanne, 1965- author.
Title: Cool cars/Erin Kelly.
Description: New York: Children's Press, an imprint of Scholastic Inc., 2020. | Series: Be an expert! | "Produced by Spooky Cheetah Press." | Audience: Grades K-1 | Summary: "Book introduces the reader to Cool Cars"—Provided by publisher.
Identifiers: LCCN 2019028541 | ISBN 9780531127636 (library binding) | ISBN 9780531132425 (paperback)
Subjects: LCSH: Automobiles—Juvenile literature. | Vehicles—Juvenile literature. | Transportation, Automotive—Juvenile literature.
Classification: LCC TL147 .K43 2020 | DDC 629.222—dc23
LC record available at https://lccn.loc.gov/2019028541

Printed in Heshan, China 62

SCHOLASTIC, CHILDREN'S PRESS, BE AN EXPERT!™, and associated logos are trademarks and/or registered trademarks of Scholastic Inc.

2 3 4 5 6 7 8 9 10 R 29 28 27 26 25 24 23 22 21 20

Scholastic Inc., 557 Broadway, New York, NY 10012.

Art direction and design by THREE DOGS DESIGN LLC.

Photos ©: cover girl and throughout: jlmatt/iStockphoto; cover road: pingebat/Shutterstock; cover fiat: Vincenzo Lombardo/Getty Images; cover mini cooper: ImageBROKER/Alamy Images; back cover car and throughout: Helgidinson/Dreamstime; spine and throughout: VanReeel/iStockphoto; 1 main: Lawrence Weslowski Jr/Dreamstime; 1 sign: FocusDzign/Shutterstock; 2 top left and throughout: Grzegorz Czapski/Shutterstock; 2 top right: Ron Kimball/KimballStock; 2 center right: KimballStock; 2 bottom left: 530897Tomas Rodriguez/Getty Images; 2 bottom right: Ron Kimball/KimballStock; 3 top left: H. Mark Weidman Photography/Alamy Images; 3 top right suv: Brian Kimball/KimballStock; 3 top right rocks and throughout: nasidastudio/Shutterstock; 3 center left: KimballStock; 3 bottom right: BoxerX/Shutterstock; 4-5 background and throughout: Arden_Panikk/Shutterstock; 4 red car: PavloBaliukh/iStockphoto; 5 boy: Seth Sanchez/Icon Sportswire/Corbis/Getty Images; 5 yellow car and throughout: GTS Productions/Shutterstock; 6-7 background: Iconic Bestiary/Shutterstock; 6-7 limo: Ron Kimball/KimballStock; 6 limo driver: RosaIreneBetancourt 13/Alamy Images; 7 boy and throughout: Maksym Topchii/Dreamstime; 8-9 police car and throughout: Roman Tiraspolsky/Alamy Images; 9 girl and throughout: ktaylorg/iStockphoto; 10-11 background: fredrisher/Shutterstock; 10 red suv: Brian Kimball/KimballStock; 11 green suv: KimballStock; 12-13 background: Cat with tail/Shutterstock; 12 bottom left: KimballStock; 12 bottom right: Ron Kimball/KimballStock; 13 all cars: KimballStock; 14 family: LightField Studios/Shutterstock; 14-15 odyssey and throughout: Teddyleung/Dreamstime; 15 hat: Susan Schmitz/Shutterstock; 15 puppy: Ethan.Films/Shutterstock; 15 family: Luca Santilli/Shutterstock; 16-17 background skyline: Nataniil/iStockphoto; 16-17: background road: Mr.Thanakorn Kotpootorn/Shutterstock; 17 waymo: Guy Bell/Alamy Images; 18-19 background: Arden_Panikk/Shutterstock; 18 all cars: Ron Kimball/KimballStock; 19 boy: JBryson/iStockphoto; 19 race car driver: Urbanandsport/NurPhoto/Getty Images; 19 nascar: David Hahn/Icon Sportswire/Getty Images; 20 limo: Ron Kimball/KimballStock; 21 child: Tomas Rodriguez/Getty Images; 21 smart car: KimballStock; 21 suv: Carlos Osorio/AP Images; 21 race car: Ron Kimball/KimballStock; 22: Chris Graythen/Getty Images; 23 gas can: nexus 7/Shutterstock; 23 hot tub: yelo34/iStockphoto; 23 race car driver: Chris Graythen/Getty Images.